When Life Makes Me Mad

KIDS HAVE *TROUBLES* TOO

A House Between Homes:
Kids in the Foster Care System

What's Going to Happen Next?
Kids in the Juvenile Court System

I Live in Two Homes:
Adjusting to Divorce and Remarriage

When My Brother Went to Prison

When Daddy Hit Mommy

My Feelings Have Names

I Don't Keep Secrets

I Like Me

When Life Makes Me Mad

A Place Called Dead

When My Sister Got Sick

When My Dad Lost His Job

Sometimes My Mom Drinks Too Much

When Life Makes Me Mad

by Sheila Stewart and Rae Simons

Mason Crest Publishers

MASON CREST PUBLISHERS INC.
370 Reed Road
Broomall, Pennsylvania 19008
(866)MCP-BOOK (toll free)
www.masoncrest.com

First Printing
9 8 7 6 5 4 3 2 1

Library of Congress Cataloging-in-Publication Data

Stewart, Sheila, 1975–
  When life makes me mad / by Sheila Stewart and Rae Simons.
       p. cm.
  Includes index.
  ISBN (set) 978-1-4222-1691-0   ISBN 978-1-4222-1700-9
  ISBN (ppbk set) 978-1-4222-1904-1   ISBN 978-1-4222-1913-3 (pbk.)
  1. Anger in children—Juvenile literature. 2. Anger—Juvenile literature. I. Simons, Rae, 1957– II. Title.
  BF723.A4S74 2011
  152.4'7—dc22

Design by MK Bassett-Harvey.
Produced by Harding House Publishing Service, Inc.
www.hardinghousepages.com
Illustrations by Russell Richardson, RxDx Productions.
Cover design by Torque Advertising + Design.
Printed in USA by Bang Printing.

The creators of this book have made every effort to provide accurate information, but it should not be used as a substitute for the help and services of trained professionals.

Introduction

Each child is unique—and each child encounters a unique set of circumstances in life. Some of these circumstances are more challenging than others, and how a child copes with those challenges will depend in large part on the other resources in her life.

The issues children encounter cover a wide range. Some of these are common to almost all children, including threats to self-esteem, anger management, and learning to identify emotions. Others are more unique to individual families, but problems such as parental unemployment, a death in the family, or divorce and remarriage are common but traumatic events in many children's lives. Still others—like domestic abuse, alcoholism, and the incarceration of a family member—are unfortunately not uncommon in today's world.

Whatever problems a child encounters in life, understanding that he is not alone is a key component to helping him cope. These books, both their fiction and nonfiction elements, allow children to see that other children are in the same situations. The books make excellent tools for triggering conversation in a nonthreatening way. They will also promote understanding and compassion in children who may not be experiencing these issues themselves.

These books offer children important factual information—but perhaps more important, they offer hope.

—*Cindy Croft, M.A., Ed., Director of the Center for Inclusive Child Care*

Lamar Phillips came in the door of his family's apartment and kicked the cat.

"Now why'd you go and do that?" his mother asked him. Her voice was sharp, but he could tell she wasn't really thinking about him. Her eyes never left the piece of paper she held in her hand.

"I'm mad," Lamar said.

"How'd you like it if I kicked YOU every time I got mad?" his mom said. She looked up from the piece of paper—Lamar thought it looked like the gas bill—and this time her eyes were looking at him. Lamar hung his head. His mom looked like she might feel like kicking him right now.

"Oh, go on with you." His mom flapped her hand at him and turned back to the bill she held in her hand. "Change out of your school clothes and go shoot some hoops. Get rid of some of those bad feelings on a basketball, instead of that poor cat that never did you any harm."

Lamar sighed. At least his mom didn't look like she was mad at HIM anymore. He went into the room he shared with his little sister Towanda.

Instantly, all his mad feelings were back. "Towanda, what are you doing with my Nintendo DS? You know I told you not to touch it!"

Towanda looked up at him, her eyes round with guilt. "I'm sorry, Lamar. I—"

But Lamar didn't feel like listening to her. He grabbed her by the shoulder and yanked her off her bed. "You little freak! I'm going to pound you—" He swung back his arm.

His mom's voice cut through the anger that was pounding inside his head. "You stop it right there, Mr. Lamar Phillips! Don't you touch your little sister!"

Lamar let his hand drop, but he was breathing hard. He wanted to say bad words. He wanted to break something. He was scared he might start crying. "It's not fair!" he burst out. "My DS is the one nice thing I own. You know how she breaks things. I HATE sharing a room with her! I hate HER!"

Towanda burst into noisy sobs and flung herself at their mother. "I didn't do anything to his stupid DS," she gulped. "He's mean. I hate HIM!"

Their mother flew her hands up in the air. "Quiet, both of you! Towanda, you shouldn't be touching Lamar's stuff. You know better. And as for you, Lamar, you need to get control of yourself right now. Take your angry self upstairs to your grandma's apartment. She needs help cleaning up all that dirt the super left behind when he fixed her pipes. Do something useful. Maybe it will help you think about someone besides yourself for a change."

"But—" Lamar started to say. What about going out to shoot some hoops? he wanted to ask her. But her expression told him he'd better not.

He trudged up the stairs to his grandma's apartment, muttering to himself. "It's not fair," he said again and again, kicking the stair treads. Two floors up, he went down the hallway and knocked on his grandmother's door.

"Hi, Grandma," he said when she opened the door. "Mom sent me up to help you clean the mess from your pipes."

His grandmother smiled at him and pulled him inside. "Boy, you look like a thundercloud. I could

use your help—but you look like you have a story to tell. What's been happening to get your lip stuck out so far?"

Lamar threw himself down on his grandma's sofa. She brought him a glass of sweet tea and a plate of oatmeal cookies she'd baked. He sighed. Nothing ever seemed quite as bad when he was with Grandma.

"Life just gets me so mad," he said.

She sat down next to him and pulled his head onto her soft shoulder. "So what happened, honey?"

Lamar took a bite of cookie. "Everything. First I got in trouble at school with the teacher. She thought I was talking while she was teaching math class—but I wasn't, it was the kid who sits behind me. And when I tried to tell her it wasn't me, she just got madder at me and yelled some more."

"That's wasn't fair, was it?"

Lamar picked up his head and looked at his grandmother. "No! It wasn't. And then when I went to the library on my way home from school and tried to take out some books, the librarian told me I couldn't because I never bring back my books on time. But I'm not the one who doesn't bring my books back, it's Towanda. She uses my library card, and then she always loses track of her books. But the librarian said it didn't matter, that I'm responsible for seeing that my little sister brings her books back if I'm going to let her use my card. But mom MAKES me let Towanda use my card, because Towanda's too little to get one on her own."

"And that's not fair either, is it?" his grandma asked quietly.

"No, it's not!"

"So what else happened today?"

"When I came in downstairs, that new kid in 101A, the big kid? He was getting his mail, and I accidentally tripped on his backpack. He grabbed me and shoved me up against the wall, and told me to stay away from his stuff."

"Were you scared?"

Lamar leaned forward and picked up his glass of tea. He took a sip and then admitted, "Yeah. I was more mad than I was scared, but I was too scared to let him see I was mad." He gave his grandma a crooked little grin. "I didn't feel like getting my nose squashed by his fist."

"No, I don't blame you. But I'll have a word with HIS grandma. I met her today down in the laundry room, and I think she'll have a word with that young man. He needs to be a little more careful with his temper. Just like another young man I know."

"Grandma, that kid is a bully," Lamar protested. "I'm not like that. I don't pick on people for no reason." He frowned, trying not to think of the little squeak the cat had made when he kicked him.

Grandma reached for her own glass of tea. "Well, it occurs to me, that large young man might have had a day very much like yours, to be flying off the handle like that so easy. What do you think?"

Lamar thought about the kid who lived downstairs. It was hard to imagine him having a bad day. Who would bother him when he was so BIG? Grandma had to be wrong about that one.

Grandma sipped her tea. "His grandma told me he has a lot of trouble at school. Learning comes hard for him, because he can't read so well. The letters get mixed up when he looks at them. She says she's sure he has some kind of learning disability and wants to get him tested, now that he's living with her and in a new school. He must get pretty frustrated." She chewed on a cookie. "And embarrassed. Scared too. Must be hard to be so big and not be able to read, don't you think?"

Lamar ate his cookie and drank his tea. "Yeah," he said finally. "Maybe."

He put his head back on his grandma's shoulder. The angry feelings inside him were starting to go away now. He'd noticed this happening before. It was like his grandmother had a magic ability to just suck the bad stuff out of him sometimes.

"So was there more? Must have been something that happened at home if your mama sent you upstairs to me."

"Yeah." Lamar sighed again. He told his grandma about the cat and then about Towanda.

His grandmother laughed. "Sounds like you and that boy down in 101A are a lot alike. It's like a chain, isn't it? Maybe your teacher was having a bad day too, or the librarian. Someone did something in their lives that wasn't fair, something they couldn't control. So they took it out on you, just like that boy did, except they yelled instead of used their hands. And then YOU got mad—and you took it out on the cat and your poor little sister. Right now, the cat is probably letting his anger out by biting off a mouse's head, and Towanda's probably slapping her doll baby."

Lamar grinned. "I guess that's the end of the angry chain, though, huh, Grandma? The mouse is dead, and the doll can't do anything."

"Don't you be fresh, boy." His grandma laughed and got to her feet. "Angry chains have a way of never ending unless you make them. Anger just keeps getting passed along and passed along—till someone decides to stop and do something different."

Lamar followed his grandma into the kitchen. "I mopped this up the best I could," she said, "but it needs to have someone take a brush to it, to get all the gunk out of the cracks."

Lamar looked at the black mess of grease and dirty water that had spilled out from under the sink and across the floor. He knew it was hard for his grandma to get down on her knees because of her arthritis. "The super shouldn't have left it like that!" he said. "He should have cleaned up after himself. It was his fault in the first place, 'cause he never comes when we tell him the pipes aren't working."

He grabbed the scrub brush his grandmother handed him and knelt down. "It's not fair! There are too many things that just aren't fair."

His grandma sat down in one of the chairs beside the kitchen table. "Boy, you're absolutely right. And it's right to speak up and say it out loud when something's not fair. You don't have to lay down and be a little limp rag that lets himself get kicked around."

Lamar looked up at his grandma. "But didn't you just tell me we have to stop being angry?"

His grandmother squinted her eyes. "It's hard to tell the difference, I admit. But there's the kind of anger that makes you kick the cat and hurt Towanda—and makes grownups scold kids without listening to their side of the story, and big boys beat up on littler boys. And then there's the kind of anger that makes you stand up and fight for what's right. That's the kind of anger that Martin Luther King Jr. had. He believed we could change things by speaking out and not hurting anyone. And he DID change things."

Lamar stood up and washed out the dirty brush at the sink, then went back to his cleaning. He scowled down at the greasy floor. "Martin Luther King got killed, Grandma. Doesn't seem like it worked out so well for him."

Grandma sighed. "No, it did not. Because one of those angry chains had been built all around him—and people just didn't want to let go of it. Martin scared them, because he was changing the world. With his life—and with his death—he did a whole lot to break the angry chains. The world's a better place now because of him."

Lamar sat back on his heels. "Grandma, I'm no Martin Luther King Jr. I don't think I can be."

She laughed. "You'd be surprised, boy. You don't think Martin ever got mad at his sister or kicked the cat when he was a boy? It takes time to learn to control our anger. But the more you practice cutting chains and building up the world instead of tying it up in chains, the easier it gets the next time. It's like shooting hoops. You'll always make mistakes—but the more you do it, the better you get."

Lamar went back to cleaning the floor. He thought about what his grandma had said. He saw Towanda's big round eyes in his mind, and he suddenly wanted to hug her. Poor little kid, he could kind of remember back when he was her age, and the way he'd always wanted to play with his cousin Lloyd's stuff. She really wasn't so bad.

Lamar scrubbed some more. He thought about the big kid in 101A. He didn't want to hug HIM—but was there a way he could talk to him sometime, he wondered. Find out if Grandma was right about him, at least?

Lamar took a rag and wiped up the last of the dirty water from the floor. He put away the scrub brush and the rag beneath the sink. Then he hugged his grandmother. "Thanks, Grandma. You got some kind of magic in you."

His grandmother hugged him back. "Thank YOU, Lamar, for helping an old lady clean her floor. You go on home now. Make your apologies to your sister and your mother. See if you can break a chain or two tonight in your family."

"Okay, Grandma." Lamar opened the door to the hallway.

"Lamar?"

Lamar turned around. "Yeah, Grandma?"

"Don't forget the cat."

You've gotten mad, haven't you? It's an emotion just about every person has felt at some time or another. And sometimes you just can't help it! Things happen that make people mad, kids and grownups, too. Getting angry, which is just another word for mad, is part of being a human being, part of the whole range of emotions—love, happiness, sadness, jealousy, fear, embarrassment—that people sometimes feel. Our emotions are an important part of making us who we are. You wouldn't be you if you didn't laugh when you thought something was funny, or cry when you felt sad. You wouldn't be you if you didn't get mad sometimes. Nice feelings—like the way you feel about your best friend or the pride of doing well on a test—and not-so-nice feelings, too (like getting angry)—they're all a part of you being you.

Understand the Word

Emotion is another word for feelings, like love, happiness, or anger.

A **process** is work that you do carefully, step-by-step.

An important part of growing up, one of the most important, is learning to understand your feelings, learning to understand why you feel them, how you act when you are feeling a certain **emotion**, and how your feelings make other people around you feel. It's a long, sometimes hard, **process** to really get

Human beings experience a lot of different emotions, both good and bad.

to know and understand yourself, but people who really work at it end up being happier and healthier people.

What Makes You Mad?

Do you know the expression to "push somebody's buttons"? It means knowing exactly how to do or say the things that make a person mad. You probably know at least a couple of people, your mom or your teacher, maybe, whose buttons you really know how to push! Think about it. What is it that you do that can make your mom mad every time you do it? What is it that, when you start doing it, your mom might ask, "Are you trying to make me mad?"

So what pushes your buttons? What is it that can happen to you or what is it that someone else does that can really make you angry? Lamar got mad at his little sister Towanda for one of the most common reasons in just about every family—she played with his stuff! Having their toys or clothes or books or whatever messed around with by somebody else, especially a brother or sister, makes a lot of kids mad.

Jealousy also makes people mad, in families, among friends, and at school. Is somebody getting treated better than you? Does somebody have something that you wish you had? Is the teacher playing favorites? Is your best friend getting too friendly with someone you don't like? Being jealous of somebody else can make a lot of kids mad.

Frustration, the feeling you get when things just aren't going the way you want them, is another common cause of anger. You don't feel in control of something, nobody seems to care how you're feeling, and the next thing you know, you're getting mad! The same thing often happens when people don't understand what you're trying to say, which can make you feel frustrated, or if they don't listen to you or act as though what you have to say is important. It can make you angry.

And don't you just hate it when something is unfair? Or when you see people you like being treated badly? Don't mean kids make you mad?

Other people not respecting your things, jealousy, frustration, other people's mean or bad behavior— there are so many things that can make a kid mad. And sometimes they can all add up and you can just be MAD—at life.

Getting frustrated over something like schoolwork can make you mad at
the world, and might make you angry at other people, too.

How Does It Make You Act?

When things aren't going the way a baby wants them to—he isn't getting his bottle as soon as he wants it or somebody takes his teddy bear away—he gets mad. He scrunches up his little face, he makes fists out of his little hands, and he cries, and cries . . . and cries. And when little kids get frustrated and angry, they lay on the floor and kick and scream and "throw a tantrum." Bigger kids and grownups sometimes feel the same way a baby or a little kid does. They may even want to cry and kick and scream, but it doesn't usually work for them. Learning to control your emotions is part of growing up—and it can be hard.

Strong emotions, like love and hate and anger, can be the hardest to learn to control. Sometimes when older kids and grownups get mad, that "little kid" still inside of them can come out. Some people cry when they get angry. They're not sad, they're mad. Some people raise their voices and yell. They can make a lot of noise letting everyone around them know they're not happy, and they can say very mean things. Some people, when they get really mad, kick and punch and throw things. They punch walls or kick the poor cat, like Lamar did. They break things and destroy other people's property. Sometimes, and this should never, ever be allowed, they hit the person they're mad at or whoever else might be around. Angry people can hurt themselves and the people around them. Some people, when they are really, really angry, cry and yell and throw things and punch all at the same time. That's

Little kids often cry when they get angry, but so do some bigger kids and adults.

Angry people can turn violent, and might take out their anger by punching the wall.

definitely the time to get as far away from them as possible! It can be scary, and people can get hurt.

Are you somebody who cries when you're mad? Do you yell? Do you throw things? Have you ever said mean things to somebody when you were angry? Have you ever hit anybody? Knowing what makes you mad and how you act when you get mad are important things to know and understand about yourself. It can help you **avoid** the things, or even the people, that make you mad—that push your buttons—and it can help you learn how to avoid acting in ways that can hurt you and other people.

How to Deal with Your Anger, and Other People's, Too

Sometimes things are just going to happen that make you mad. Sometimes, little things that have made you feel frustrated and angry during the day can add up and you might get really mad about something that's really not so bad. That's what happened to Lamar in our story. He was having a bad day, and it was adding up. Life was making him mad and he expressed his anger by taking it out on

Understand the Word

Avoid means to keep away from something.

You have to learn how to deal with people who push your buttons. The goal is to get control over your own emotions, and not to let other people control them.

his cat and his little sister. His mother was busy paying the bills, but she could see that he was having a "mad at the world day," and her first suggestion was a very good one—that Lamar go out and play some basketball. Sometimes exercise, even just taking a walk, can get your mind off your anger and help you put your energy into something besides being mad, something that's good for you. But it was too late for shooting hoops to help Lamar deal with his anger once he started fighting with his sister and getting ready to hit her. Luckily his mom had a place to send him—upstairs to his grandma's apartment. Spending some time with his grandmother was exactly what Lamar needed. She let him tell her what was bothering him, she listened, and she helped him feel **calmer** and ready to apologize—say he was sorry—to the people (and pet) he had been mean to when he was mad.

Not all angry kids are lucky enough to have a kind, understanding grandmother right upstairs, but most of us have a grownup or a friend our age who knows us well enough, and cares enough about us, to understand what might be making us mad, someone who

Understand the Word

To be **calmer** means to be more peaceful, quieter, and happier.

will listen to us, and help calm us down. A lot of times, talking about your feelings is the best way to keep your anger from building up to the point where you really get mad and start saying and doing things you might be sorry for later. Friends, family members, and school counselors can all be good people for you to talk with about your angry feelings, and doing this can really help. If you're the kind of kid who gets mad and hurts people, either with words or with your hands, or who hurts yourself, it's very important that you try to learn to control your anger and keep yourself and other people safe. Again, a caring grownup, like a counselor, a teacher, or a doctor could really help you.

Understand the Word

To **express** something is to put your feelings into words or actions.

Some kids really have things to be mad about: parents who fight, older brothers or sisters who use drugs, being bullied by other kids, being hurt or abused by adults. And sad things can make you mad, too. If your mom is sick, let's say, your worrying about her, being scared, and feeling helpless can **express** itself in anger. You might not even know what's making you mad sometimes, but it can just be the way your mind is trying to deal with your problems.

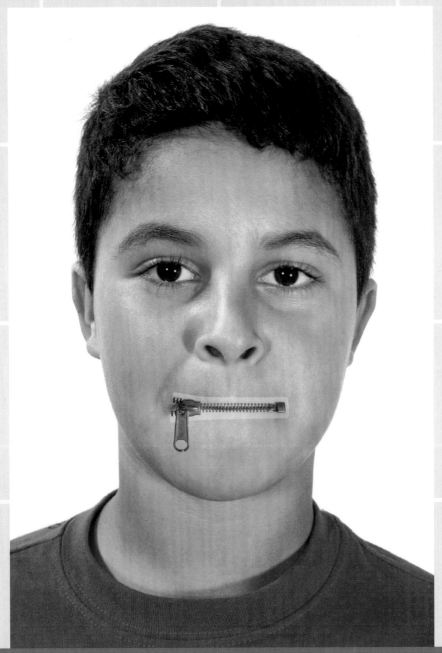

Don't feel like you have to keep your mouth closed about feeling angry. It helps to talk about it with a trusted adult or friend.

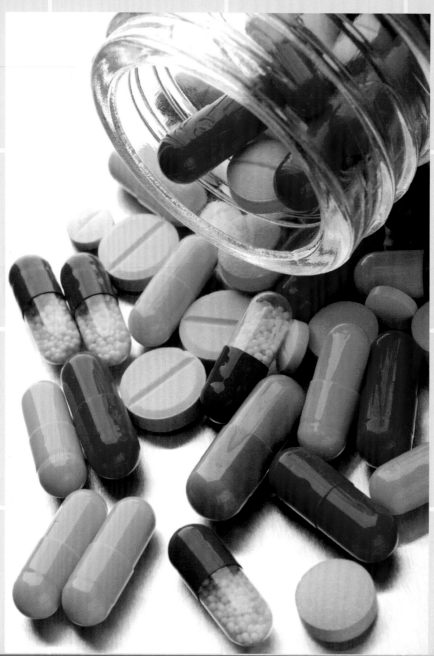

Problems at home, like if one of your parents or siblings uses illegal drugs, can make you very angry, for good reason.

Feeling angry all the time is not good for you, and no kid should have to feel that way. Talk to someone who can help you. It might be scary to talk about such strong emotions, but it's the very best thing you can do to help yourself.

Learning to deal with your own anger is hard enough; dealing with somebody else's anger can be even harder. Some kids you know may have a problem with anger. They can hurt and bully other kids, and they might pick on you some times. Some adults have grown up without ever learning how to control how they act when they get mad. Drinking alcohol or taking drugs can sometimes make grownups get mad easily, and they can take it out on kids. Some parents get mad for reasons that their kids don't even understand, and they yell at them and hit them. This can be very, very scary for a kid.

Remember, you should never, ever let another kid or a grownup hurt you, even if it's somebody like your mom or dad whom you love very much. When a person around you is getting angry and starts doing things that scare you or hurt you in any way, get away as fast as you can. Tell a grownup who can help, call the police if you think you might be in danger, do whatever you need to do to be safe and away from any angry person who might hurt you.

Getting mad can be scary. You can scare yourself by getting out of control and saying and doing things that are mean and hurt the people around you and yourself, too. And being around loud, violent angry people can be scary and dangerous.

When Life Makes You Mad

Getting mad once in a while is part of being you. It happens to everybody. A lot of times it's better to express your anger by talking about it than to hold it in and let it build up. Built-up anger can be a very bad thing because when it finally comes out, it can hurt you and other people. So try to talk about what's making you mad before the feeling gets too strong to handle. The best people to talk to are those people who know you and know how to help you deal with problems, who can help you calm yourself down.

Get to know yourself. Know what makes you mad and how being mad makes you act. Try to avoid the things and the people that make you mad. Think before you speak when you're angry. Try not to say

It's not OK if your parent is so angry that he or she hits you.

If you keep all your anger inside you, it's liable to explode out at some point.

things you'll be sorry for later. Never ever hit or kick or punch a person when you get mad or do anything to hurt yourself. Take a walk, read a book, get your mind off being mad. Put your energy into something that's fun and interesting and good for you. But if you do get mad, make sure you're ready to say you're sorry to the people around you. Angry people can scare other people and hurt their feelings.

If somebody around you is mad and acting scary or dangerous, get away from him as quickly as you can. Go to a grownup you can trust and keep yourself safe at all times.

Sure, you and the people in your life and around you are going to get mad sometimes. But the world would be a happier place if everybody tried not to get too mad too often!

Questions to Think About

1. What are some of the things that really make you mad?

2. Describe how you act when you get angry.

3. Do you think you've ever hurt anybody's feelings or scared them when you were mad at them?

4. Do you have any ways to "calm yourself down" when you feel yourself getting mad?

Further Reading

Huebner, Dawn. *What to Do When Your Temper Flares: A Kid's Guide to Overcoming Problems with Anger.* New York: Magination, 2007.

Verdick, Elizabeth. *How to Take the Grr Out of Anger.* New York: Free Spirit, 2002.

Wilde, Jerry. *Hot Stuff to Help Kids Chill Out: The Anger Management Book.* New York: LGR Publishing, 2007.

Find Out More on the Internet

Anger Management
www.angriesout.com/

Taking Charge of Anger
kidshealth.org/kid/feeling/emotion/anger.html

The websites listed on this page were active at the time of publication. The publisher is not responsible for websites that have changed their address or discontinued operation since the date of publication. The publisher will review and update the websites upon each reprint.

Index

Picture Credits

air_s; fotolia: p. 42
Coburn, Stephen; fotolia: p. 37
crabshack photos; fotolia: p. 29
gemenacom; fotolia: p. 33
godfer; fotolia: p. 41

Mannaggia; fotolia: p. 26
milo sluz; fotolia: p. 38
Svara, Lisa; fotolia: p. 31
zimmytws; fotolia: p. 32

To the best knowledge of the publisher, all images not specifically credited are in the public domain. If any image has been inadvertently uncredited, please notify Harding House Publishing Service, 220 Front Street, Vestal, New York 13850, so that credit can be given in future printings.

About the Authors

Sheila Stewart has written several dozen books for young people, both fiction and nonfiction, although she especially enjoys writing fiction. She has a master's degree in English and now works as a writer and editor. She lives with her two children in a house overflowing with books, in the Southern Tier of New York State.

Rae Simons is a freelance author who has written numerous educational books for children and young adults. She also has degrees in psychology and special education, and she has worked with children encountering a range of troubles in their lives.

About the Consultant

Cindy Croft, M.A. Ed., is Director of the Center for Inclusive Child Care, a state-funded program with support from the McKnight Foundation, that creates, promotes, and supports pathways to successful inclusive care for all children. Its goal is inclusion and retention of children with disabilities and behavioral challenges in community child care settings. Cindy Croft is also on the faculty at Concordia University, where she teaches courses on young children with special needs and the emotional growth of young children. She is the author of several books, including *The Six Keys: Strategies for Promoting Children's Mental Health.*